VIVIANA MOLINA

Heal Heartbreak in 5 Steps

Advice and practical exercises to transform your heartbreak into breakthroughs

Copyright © 2024 by Viviana Molina

All rights reserved. No part of this publication may be reproduced, stored or transmitted in any form or by any means, electronic, mechanical, photocopying, recording, scanning, or otherwise without written permission from the publisher. It is illegal to copy this book, post it to a website, or distribute it by any other means without permission.

Viviana Molina asserts the moral right to be identified as the author of this work.

Viviana Molina has no responsibility for the persistence or accuracy of URLs for external or third-party Internet Websites referred to in this publication and does not guarantee that any content on such Websites is, or will remain, accurate or appropriate.

Designations used by companies to distinguish their products are often claimed as trademarks. All brand names and product names used in this book and on its cover are trade names, service marks, trademarks and registered trademarks of their respective owners. The publishers and the book are not associated with any product or vendor mentioned in this book. None of the companies referenced within the book have endorsed the book.

First edition

This book was professionally typeset on Reedsy.
Find out more at reedsy.com

Contents

Introduction

Understanding our attachment styles, relationship patterns, emotional triggers and trauma wounds is fundamental for creating healthy and long-lasting relationships. We often find ourselves replaying a romantic novel or mexican novela within our relationships thinking that this is the way relationships should be; filled with pain, emotional suffering and a deep sense of longing, abandonment and rejection. In fact, we can choose not to engage in these relationship patterns with confidence, grace, trust, a deep sense of self love and clear consistent boundaries. Choosing to move away from these unhealthy relationships or "trauma bonding" does not have to be emotionally painful as long as you have resolved your childhood trauma wounds that are being projected as emotional triggers.

The objective of this book is to help you move away from emotional codependency by understanding the psychology and theory behind it (this will give you a sense of grounding and knowing that your issue is solvable), reprogramming the subconscious mind through meditation and journalling, establishing clear boundaries by committing to this process, putting into practice choosing the right partner for you and moving away from the wrong partners or suitors.

You will benefit from this course if you...

- are constantly being emotionally triggered in relationships.
- feel intense emotional pain, sadness, grief, anger, shame, rejection, abandonment when not in a relationship.
- feel that your relationship is unhealthy, but you can't seem to detach or move away from it
- constantly feel abandoned, rejected and unloved
- constantly feel needy and a lack of physical and emotional affection
- are constantly obsessing over a crush, romantic interest or ex-partner.
- repeat patterns in relationships that leave you feeling depleted and unloved.
- engage in unhealthy behaviors like chasing or being too sexually or emotionally available.
- crave emotional intimacy but worry that others don't want the same with you.
- recognize that being in an intimate relationship tends to take over your life and you become overly fixated on the other person.
- may find it difficult to observe boundaries, viewing space between you as a threat, something that can provoke panic, anger, or fear that your partner no longer wants you.
- tend to place a lot of your sense of self-worth on how you feel you're being treated in the relationship, and you tend to overreact to any perceived threats to the relationship.
- feel anxious or jealous when away from your partner and may use guilt, controlling behavior, or other manipulative tactics to keep them close.
- need constant reassurance and lots of attention from your

partner.

- notice that others may criticize you for being too needy or clingy and you may struggle to maintain close relationships.

HOW THE ACTIVITIES WITHIN THIS BOOK WILL BE DEVELOPED

Each chapter will be developed with the following elements:

Psychoeducation: You will be provided with information and tools about psychological concepts. In each section you will learn about mental health topics such as attachment styles, trauma bonding and subconscious reprogramming.

Tools: You will implement some techniques to recognize and manage emotional difficulties that involve written exercises and art therapy activities.

Art Therapy: You will use artistic materials to express thoughts, feelings and emotions and comprehend how the creative process can create emotional well-being. Art Therapy is a discipline in the field of psychotherapy in which artistic resources are used for therapeutic purposes. It consists of performing simple art exercises that will allow you to express thoughts, feelings and emotions through non-verbal language. The objective of the workshop is to create emotional well-being through psychoeducation and the creative process.

Guided Meditations: These meditations use hypnosis and neural reprogramming to create new neural pathways in the brain by changing limiting beliefs to empowered and positive beliefs. Through daily reinforcement these meditations will allow you to calm the symptoms of dysregulation brought on by childhood attachment wounds being projected in present day situations. You will find these in youtube.

WHAT YOU WILL NEED

To develop these workshops effectively, you will need a pen, a notebook, pad or journal, headphones, a good internet connection. Set aside time and space for learning and doing the meditations. Choose a space and a time where you will not be interrupted, and you can be quiet for several minutes. For the meditations you can use an eye pad, a blanket and essential oils such as lavender or thyme. There are a lot of written exercises to develop throughout this workshop. If writing is not something that you would like to do, then you can record your voice on your phone and play it back for you.

DISCLAIMER OF LIABILITY

The activities contained within this book are a complement to improve your mental health and wellbeing. They allow you an educational space on themes related to mental health and emotional well-being. Emotional wellness activities are not a substitute for any medical or therapeutic treatment related to mental health. If you have a mental health illness you should seek the support of a psychologist, psychiatrist or therapist.

I

THE PSYCHOLOGY BEHIND ATTACHMENT

1

Understanding emotional codependency

Emotional codependency is the emotional or psychological dependency or reliance that a person can have on a partner, crush, romantic interest, family member or coworker. Basically, any person that you are in a relationship with.

The term "Codependency" was initially used to define a person who has addictive behaviors towards an illegal substance. These behaviors are typically characterized by the inability to disengage or detach from the substance despite its obvious and recognizable harmful effects on the user's body, mental health, well-being, and overall life. Codependency in substance abuse points out the user's need for the substance to function in their lives. Addicts report feeling lost, confused, unable to make decisions and feel whole without their drug.

Emotional codependency functions in a very similar way. Codependents feel they need another to feel emotionally stable, make decisions, feel whole or have a sense of purpose in their lives. These two scenarios (drug addict and emotional addict), are very similar and have a similar psychological basis (with obvious inherent differences in prognosis, treatments etc...) A deep emotional void is looking to be filled via an outside source instead of being resolved internally. Go through the list below and highlight the traits or behaviors that you identify with.

You are emotionally codependent if in a relationship you:

- constantly monitor your partners level of availability, interest, and responsiveness
- constantly grasp for the relationship or feel that it is slipping out of your hands.
- hyper focus on the other.
- over adapt and over function to preserve the connection.
- are frequently consumed by fears of abandonment.
- give up your own needs or sense of self.
- yield to the needs of your partner to ensure proximity and relationship security.
- jump into relationships or bond very quickly with people.
- idealize your partner to the point of making excuses for their bad behavior.
- are anxious and controlling.
- have feelings of not being enough.
- obsessively thinking of the relationship or the other person.
- have obsessive and controlling thoughts.
- obsessively check your phone for messages.
- are relentlessly daydreaming.
- are overanalyzing or over thinking.
- are reading into everything.

- feel like this person has hijacked your nervous system.
- are emotionally invested in a person you barely know.
- define your mood, happiness, and identity according to what the other says or does.
- change your mood, actions, thinking and behavior because of the other person.
- define yourself by your relationship and will do whatever it takes to stay in it.
- the thought of your partner leaving you sends you into a spiral of pain and confusion.
- are uncomfortable, or even terrified of being alone.
- become demanding, possessive, or needy for approval, re-assurance, contact or greater emotional or sexual intensity.

- **WRITTEN EXERCISE**

Do you recognize any of these patterns in the way you behave or feel in relationships? Write four headings (emotional, physical, cognitive and behavioral). Under each heading write how you feel emotionally, physically, what are your thought patterns, and how you behave in your relationships. Do you see a pattern? What is your relational pattern? Do you tend to chase and grasp at relationships rather than choosing and selecting what feels right for you based on what it means to be in a healthy relationship? Do you tend to chase relationships or make yourself too available?

2

Attachment styles

I f you have identified yourself as being codependent then you will most likely have an **anxious ambivalent attachment style.**

Attachment styles are the ways in which, as children we learned how to love, care for, bond or attach to others through how our parents or main caregivers loved, cared for us or bonded with us. So, we basically learned how to relate to others through how our parents or caregivers related to us. These attachment patterns were imprinted into our subconscious and we integrated them as true beliefs.

Children think in absolutes and their whole world is based on what mom and dad provide for them. So, if a child is neglected or not listened to, then they will learn that they are not worthy of being cared for or listened to and they create a belief system based on their environment and how others relate to them. These types of behaviors have a tremendous impact on how we relate to others in our adult lives. Attachment styles impact all type of relationships, friendships, coworkers, bosses, family, partnerships, etc.

According to John Bowlby (1983), there are four types of attachment styles: Anxious ambivalent, Secure, Anxious Avoidant, Disorganized.

A **secure attachment style** comes from a childhood in which love, affection and satisfaction of a child's needs are consistently given. A child feels safe, seen and known, feels comfort and reassurance, valued, supported to explore. Parents are emotionally attuned to the child's needs; when they reach out they are met with care, support and affection. This teaches the child that allowing themselves to feel their needs and communicating them to others is an effective strategy. Routines are implemented and the child knows what to expect.

As adults they give and receive love in equal amounts and will withdraw from any relationship that they feel does not fully satisfy their needs. They tend to feel safe, stable, and more satisfied in their close relationships. While they don't fear being on their own, they usually thrive in close meaningful relationships. People with a secure attachment style are more flexible when their needs are not met and are able to wait or find alternatives means of having their attachment needs met without shaking the foundation of the relationship.

An **avoidant attachment style** comes from a childhood were love and affection was not given but rather withheld. Parents were mostly unavailable, neglectful or absent. In essence, the absence of physical or emotional presence from parents. Children would have experienced parenting that is cold, distant, critical or highly focused on achievement learn that they are better off relying on themselves. Parents would have exhibited expressive dissonance; when someone's facial or verbal expressions are mismatched with their emotional state, such as smiling when they are actually upset. On the other hand, parents who are overly emotional, needy or clingy and use the child as a crutch for their own emotional or physical needs. The child feels overwhelmed by the parent and learns that others are not reliable and weak and subsequently uninterested in their own needs. Therefore, they decide that it is safer not to rely on anyone else. As adults they tend to withdraw from relationships and value their independence above anything else. They don't share emotions and feel uncomfortable when others share their emotions with them. Their autonomy, independence and self-sufficiency are very important to them and therefore are uncomfortable with close relationships. They feel uncomfortable relying on partners or with partners relying on them.

A **disorganized attachment style** comes from a childhood were trauma such as emotional neglect or abuse was experienced. For example, violent caregivers with drug and alcohol addiction. Parents who are in an emotional rollercoaster, or who have drastic fluctuations in their mood. Family chaos; factors such as illness, financial instability, job insecurity or just a general lack of stability within the household. The child might have experienced some type of abuse and therefore, the emotional response that this child has towards their parents or caregivers is fear. This puts the child in a paradoxical situation, where their caretaker, who is supposed to be the source of their comfort and the solution to their fears, is the source of their fear instead. Therefore, two systems of attachment are being activated within the child: a moving towards and a protective defensive of moving away from. As adults, people with a disorganized attachment style tend to engage in risky behaviors and will be explosive in their emotional responses. They will find emotional relationships confusing and unsettling often swinging between emotional extremes of love and hate for a partner (ie. swinging between avoidant and ambivalent attachment styles). They don't feel safe and fully trusting in relationships, even if their partner acts in trustworthy ways. They genuinely want intimacy and closeness but feel overwhelmed and fearful when intimacy with a partner increases. They can frequently experience the conflicting internal drives of wanting to be close and share themselves but fearing that closeness and vulnerability will be dangerous or cause the relationship to end. Adults with disorganized attachment styles tend to have lots of sexual partners but don't engage in long term relationships. They crave the attachment and the closeness but fear being vulnerable in a relationship.

- **DISCLAIMER**

Attachment styles can change according to your relationship experiences at work, with friends, family or partner and according to your life experiences. There are social, cultural, and economic factors that also affect your attachment style. Therefore, it is a psychological and emotional phenomenon that is organic, and it changes and fluctuates according to your

circumstances and context.

ANXIOUS AMBIVALENT ATTACHMENT STYLES

An **anxious ambivalent attachment style** comes from a childhood in which love, and affection are inconsistently given. Parental behavior towards the child will be either overly intrusive and affectionate or unavailable and distant. Parents of children with this type of attachment style would have also been distracted or aloof to their child's needs because they were dealing with their own emotional difficulties or work/life responsibilities and would neglect the child to take care of themselves or their responsibilities. At other times the parent would have shown affection, care, and attention to then go back to being unavailable.

For example, the parent who is very busy working to support the household and will have limited attention for their child. Within that limited attention time the parent will engage, be playful and give too much attention to the child. Or for example, the parent who is dealing with emotional difficulties and has limited emotional bandwidth for the child so they will be emotionally and physically unavailable and emotionally and physically available when their emotions subside or level out. Because love and attention are inconsistently given, meaning it can come and be taken away at any time without warning, children will see love, affection, and attention as something that needs to be secured and controlled. Children become anxious when the parent leaves and angry when they return, fearing the imminent abandonment but weary and overwhelmed by their attention, stuck in the cycle of fearing abandonment but also fearing attention because it will be then taken away at any time. Children act in angry and jealous ways to secure their parents love and attention or a as a way of calling their attention.

These patterns play out in adult relationships as controlling, needy, and suspicious of a partners love and commitment. Review the list in the first slide for the full range of adult behaviors.

As you explore the different types of attachment styles you will notice that you may have a little of each but your tendency will gravitate to one particular attachment style. Attachment styles tend to change over time and with each relationship we experience. Take an attachment style quiz to find out your attachment style. https://dianepooleheller.com/attachment-test/

This book is for those who feel a strong tendency towards an anxious ambivalent attachment style.

· **WRITTEN EXERCISE**

Which attachment style are you? Do you have a little of each or have tendency towards a particular one? How did your parents or caregivers show you affection in childhood? Where they present, caring and affectionate? Where they cold and distant? What was the relationship with your mother like growing up? What was the relationship with your father like growing up? Was there a moment in childhood that you remember as hurtful or painful when relating to your parents or caregivers? What are your strengths and weaknesses in relationships?

3

Trauma Bonding

When choosing a partner or relationship our attachment styles strongly influence who we pick and why and the dynamics of the relationship. When we choose a partner, we are choosing them mainly based on what we learned from our parents or primary caregivers. What we registered in childhood as "love and affection" becomes our blueprint for how we relate to and choose our partners, so we base our decision upon the principle of familiarity. However, this does not mean that the way we are behaving, or the partners we choose, make up a healthy relationship.

The fact that we have chosen a partner based on the principle of familiarity and not based on the principle of what is healthy relating could mean that we have created a trauma bond with that person. If the relationship is emotionally painful, distressing, and abusive but you can't seem to get out of it then this is a clear sign that the relationship is based on a trauma bond and not care, affection and trust. Trauma bonding happens when the relationship you are in feels constantly emotionally painful, abusive, confusing, and disorientating but you can't seem to get out of it. It becomes difficult to see the alternatives and the emotional distress of abandoning the relationship is too painful to face.

If you identify that you are in a trauma bonded relationship, please seek help immediately so that you can stop enduring this type of abuse. If you feel that you are not in an abusive relationship but still feel unhappy and can't come to terms with the idea of leaving the relationship or it is too painful to leave, this can also mean that you have created a trauma bond with your partner. It is very important that at this stage you consider alternatives like individual therapy or couple's therapy.

· **WRITTEN EXERCISE**

Do you feel like you are in a trauma bonded relationship? Write freely about the things that make you feel unhappy, stressed, annoyed, sad, angry or frustrated about your relationship. Do they seem emotionally, psychologically, or physically abusive? Write freely about the things that make you feel happy, relaxed, calm, safe, secure, and cared for in your relationship. Are there more negative things than positive things? Think about your ideal relationship. If you could have anything you wanted in your relationship, what would it be?

· **ART THERAPY ACTIVITY**

Draw an image that represents your relationship at this moment.

· **WRITTEN EXERCISE**

Write what thoughts feelings and emotions came up for you during the artistic process. How does the image you drew represent your relationship?

II

COMMITMENT TO THE PROCESS AND BOUNDARIES

4

Boundaries

You may have already left a relationship, be in the process of finding a new one, grieving a past one or in the process of understanding the difficulties in your current relationship. Wherever you may be it is important to implement clear boundaries and commit to this process in order to find emotional relief from codependency symptoms. However, if you continue to be in a trauma bonded relationship or a relationship that does not make you happy, you will not be able to heal from these symptoms completely as you will be experiencing abusive behaviors from your partner while trying to heal.

Boundaries are verbal, physical, or behavioral actions that you take to let others know what you can accept or can't accept in your life and in your relationships. For example, telling someone to please let you know in advance when they want to come by your house and visit is a boundary. You are communicating to them that it is not O.K. for you when they show up unannounced. If others respect your boundaries, then they respect you, your space and time. These actions will make your nervous system feel safe and calm whenever you are around this person. If others don't respect your boundaries, then they don't respect you and this is a sign that you should take distance from this person until you feel your boundaries are being respected and you feel safe around them.

You also have to establish clear boundaries with yourself, your body and your actions. In order to detach from a codependent relationship, you must establish clear boundaries. These will include the following.

· DON'T ENGAGE SEXUALLY

Don't engage sexually with a partner who has not shown you respect, consistency, safety, and trust over a period of six weeks or more. This step is so important in detaching and working through codependent symptoms. When you engage sexually your body produces many hormones that create a feeling of bonding and deep attachment, especially for women. The hormones that are created in your body are oxytocin, dopamine, vasopressin, and prolactin for women. Men release testosterone and produce estrogen which makes them want to retreat and take some time alone. When they produce testosterone, they inhibit oxytocin, making them seek sex but not attachment; and this is why men don't bond through sex. Women, on the other hand become attached through a larger production of oxytocin. In addition to this, the part of our brain that is involved in decision making, our frontal lobe, shuts down while the part of our brain that is involved in desire and motivation, the limbic system, becomes activated. Having an orgasm stimulates the brain in the same way as drugs or other pleasurable experiences. So, you are basically letting your brain and body attach to someone who may not be the right partner for you. It then makes it even harder to detach from them. If you do choose to have sex with someone before getting to know them on a deeper level, then be very aware that the resulting feeling of attachment is not about "love and meant to be" it is largely due to your hormones and it can be very difficult to differentiate between the two; especially when you are setting boundaries, choosing the right partner and working through codependency and attachment issues relating to childhood trauma.

· GIVE THEM 6 WEEKS

This is also a very crucial boundary that is linked with not engaging sexually. If you think that you or your partner have a chance at making things work or are in the process of dating someone, give the relationship and your partner or potential love interest time to show you their interest in working things out or being the right fit for you. If over a period of six weeks you see that things don't work out, then you must let them go. If there is potential to move things forward and you feel comfortable and safe within the relationship, then you can get closer and become more vulnerable sexually and emotionally. Give yourself time and space to make rational decisions based on your emotional needs rather than on your hormonal needs. In section 3, "Finding your Ideal Partner," you will be guided step by step through the process of choosing the right partner for you, while identifying what a healthy relationship is, dating and seeing potential red flags.

· DON'T CHASE SEEK OR MANIPULATE SITUATIONS

Don't chase, seek or manipulate situations so that you can see or be around the person you want to detach from. This is the hardest boundary to implement because codependents essentially feel they can't live without their partner or love interest so the idea of not being around them can seem life threatening and emotionally painful. Ironically codependents typically enter a dynamic where they choose and avoidant partner so it feels like they are being abandoned and not being chosen and instead *they* are doing the chasing and choosing, which can be incredibly draining and painful when your effort and intentions are no being reciprocated. Avoidant partners will not make an effort, chase or work things out so don't expect them to change once you have decided to walk away. However, it is this feeling of abandonment or not being good enough that must be worked through to understand your codependent patterns and heal from its symptoms.

· DON'T ENGAGE THROUGH SOCIAL MEDIA

This includes looking at their posts, stories, commenting or liking their pictures. If you are constantly looking at their pictures and fantasizing, then it will become very difficult to detach because your energy and time will be invested in them instead of moving away from them. These are little steps that make a big difference. If you have to block or delete their number, then do so to avoid the temptation of contacting them again.

· IF IT'S MEANT TO BE IT WILL BE

A healthy relationship will develop in alignment with feeling safe, secure and cared for. Being in partnership with someone is meant to be easy and in flow. The relationship will develop in a way that feels safe for you. You will not feel the need to "fight for their love" but instead you will have a feeling of reciprocity in terms of time, energy, communication and emotional vulnerability that both parties are equally investing into the relationship. It will not feel like someone is doing all the work while the other one isn't.

· TAKE DISTANCE

Overall if a person is not enhancing your life in ways that are healthy and balanced then they are not the right person for you. It is important to trust your intuition to know what doesn't feel right and move away from them in any way you can. You can start with little steps like not looking at their social media as often or spending more time alone or with friends and family. This will give you time and space to understand your codependency patterns and work through your symptoms.

· DO THE WORK

If you identified that you are experiencing codependency patterns you will most likely need to work through recognizing childhood traumas with a therapist coach or through this process. As long as you keep recognizing these patterns, working through your emotions as well as observing the boundaries stated above, you will be healing from codependency. This person or experience is triggering a childhood wound than is putting you into a fight, flight or freeze state. These triggers need to be worked through to overcome the symptoms of codependency.

· TRUST THE PROCESS

This process takes you through rewiring the way you bond and choose partners and through changing beliefs at a subconscious level so it will take time for you to see the results. Be patient with yourself as a lot of emotional baggage will come to the surface and you will need to work through this day by day. Facing your emotional triggers and anxiety will not be easy but it will be all worth it in the end. I promise that your symptoms will be lifted, and you will be able to emotionally detach from this person with time and dedication. Trusting is a big part of this process. It's like learning a new language, it will feel unfamiliar the beginning and the right words and sentences will not flow but with practice and repetition it will al become possible.

· **WRITTEN EXERCISE**

What boundaries are difficult for you to keep? Are these boundaries that you need to set for yourself or for the other person? Can you identify how these boundaries showed up for you in childhood or in past relationships? Can you identify how you might have felt your boundaries disrespected as a child?

· **ART THERAPY ACTIVITY**

Draw an image that represents your boundaries. Are they permeable, flexible, or rigid? Do they shift and change according to the circumstances?

· **WRITTEN EXERCISE**

What thoughts came up for you during this process? What does your image represent?

III

DEALING WITH THE SYMPTOMS

5

Identify the symptoms

Now that you have started to implement boundaries and take distance from your partner/ love interest you will most likely begin to feel the codependency symptoms that have been listed above with more intensity or more will start to show up. Symptoms can vary from person to person. Some of the symptoms are listed below. Make a note or highlight the ones you are presenting at this moment.

- anxious and controlling
- have feelings of not being enough
- feel intense emotional pain, sadness, grief, anger, shame, rejection, abandonment etc.
- obsessively thinking of the relationship or the other person
- are overly excited/ have out of body euphoria.
- have obsessive and controlling thoughts.
- obsessively check your phone for messages
- are unable to concentrate.
- don't sleep well

- are relentlessly daydreaming.
- are overanalyzing or over thinking.
- reading into everything
- generally, it feels like this person has hijacked your nervous system
- are emotionally invested in a person you barely know.
- define your mood, happiness and identity according to what the other says or does
- change your mood, actions, thinking and behavior because of the other person.
- define yourself by your relationship and will do whatever it takes to stay in it.
- The thought of your partner leaving you sends you into a spiral of pain and confusion.

These symptoms can be equated to the withdrawal symptoms experienced by a drug addict when they are trying to quit their addiction. It is not an easy task, and it will be easier for some and more challenging for others.

In the attempt of finding relief from these symptoms you may relapse into codependent relationship patterns where you continue to seek the avoidant or abusive partner, engage in a pattern of choosing emotionally unavailable or avoidant partners, or engage in casual sexual relationships where you are seeking temporary validation, care and affection.

Whatever your pattern may be, engaging in relationships without doing the work of recognizing your trauma wounds and emotional codependency patterns that will eventually enable you to pick the right partner, will always put you back into square one. Where you are either left feeling abandoned and rejected or in a relationship that feels unsafe, inconsistent, and emotionally painful.

This does not mean you have to wait until you are perfect package and completely healed to date or talk to someone. Nobody is perfect and we are all constantly working through issues and difficulties in our lives. You may wish to take some time out for yourself to begin this process and continue to date and work through difficulties with your partner, as long as you follow the boundaries and stick to this process. See the Boundaries chapter and the **"Finding your Ideal Partner"** section for more guidance.

Boundaries

1. Don't engage sexually
2. Give them 6 weeks
3. Don't chase seek or manipulate situations
4. Don't engage through social media
5. If it's meant to be it will be
6. Take distance
7. Do the work
8. Commit to the process
9. Trust the process

CHAPTER 6 – SELF CARE, SELF LOVE, SELF WORTH

When I was going through codependency symptoms, I would

find dozens of blogs and videos that would suggest self-care and self-love as the cure, answer or alternative for codependency. They would suggest engaging in hobbies and activities that would take up a lot of time (cleaning the house, organizing your wardrobe, reading, putting together a puzzle etc.), going on a trip, going out with friends or family, taking up a new hobby, joining a club or online community, focusing on your work, projects etc. Self-care was portrayed as going to a spa, doing yoga, meditating, or giving yourself a facial. Needless to say, I tried all of these things and ended up in the same place, with a deep sense of loneliness, longing, abandonment, obsessive thinking and craving affection from that one person.

However, once I understood the true meaning of these concepts I began to integrate them within my practice. They were not the solution* but a beacon of light guiding me forward. I still practice them today and they have become a useful tool for healthy everyday living. Essentially, I learned that I come first. So let's get started with defining them and you can use the written exercises to keep you accountable putting yourself first!

*the solution lies with changing subconscious beliefs about yourself through neural reprogramming and healing attachment wounds.

Self-care: Basically, taking care of your whole self. This means attending to the needs of your, body, your mind, your emotions, and your general wellbeing. Doing this implies doing these things for yourself without the expectation of others doing it for you. It means being attuned to your needs and doing what is necessary to provide yourself with what you need. These actions may look like preparing healthy meals, going to the doctor for a checkup, organizing and tidying your home, saving money for a rainy day, journaling your thoughts, sleeping well, starting and exercise routine, reading a book, doing a creative activity, going to therapy etc. Self-care also means staying away from situations and people that can cause you harm or discomfort, setting healthy boundaries and protecting yourself.

Self-love: The easiest way to remember self-love is by imagining that you are the parent of your inner child and that you want to provide this inner child with the best possible experience in life. So, ask yourself what would your inner child need in this situation? How can you care for them in this moment? What decision would you make if you were thinking about her best interests? This allows you to go to a place of love and protection for yourself. This means putting yourself first by making space to prioritize your needs through showing kindness and compassion towards yourself even when you struggle and doubt yourself. When you start practicing self-love you feel that you can give more to others instead of feeling depleted and tired.

Self-worth: Self-worth relates to self-esteem and deservingness. If you have low self-esteem or low self-worth you will easily accept anything that is given to you without choosing or deciding if this is what you really want. Knowing that you deserve better or that something is not up to your standards, and you will not settle, will keep yourself worth high. When you gravitate towards people, places, things, or experiences that are uplifting, enhance your life in positive ways and provide you with nurturing, a sense of happiness and value you know that you are in your total authentic self-worth, you feel deserving of great things in life. And when something comes along that does not match your level of worth you don't engage with it. Instead, you strive for something better or look for something that is aligned to your level of deservingness. This concept is key when moving away from unfulfilling relationships.

· **WRITTEN EXERCISE**

Emotions can be overwhelming you at this point and it is important to take some time dealing with them instead of pushing them out of the way or ignoring them.

Answer the following questions in your Journal.

- What emotion is this person, situation, or event triggering inside me?
- Why is this emotion being triggered? What do I feel I am lacking within myself in this situation? (i.e., respect, to be seen fully, acceptance, communication, equality, love, affection, safety, to be heard, security, appreciation etc.)
- Where in my life have I most needed this and from whom? (i.e. in childhood, in adolescence, or early twenties)
- Can I trace this need back to a specific memory where it was very apparent and painful?
- Why do I still shrink, settle, and stay small in this area of my life? How can I give myself what I need?

· WRITTEN EXERCISE

Write everything that comes to mind about them, your relationship, romantic crush or ex-partner. How did you meet? What happened so that the relationship didn't work out? What do you like or admire about them? How do they treat you? What is confusing about how they treat you? Think about your ideal relationship. If you could have anything you wanted in your relationship, what would it be?

CHAPTER 7 - EMOTIONAL CLEARING

At this point you most likely will be feeling confused and a lot of emotional pain or some emotional pain. It is important to level your mind and body to a place where it feels calm and safe. This is called the "rest and digest" state, where the Central Nervous System is calm enough to engage and absorb new information. Codependents usually place a lot of energy and thought into the other person while leaving little room for their own needs and desires. The first step to healing is awareness and the second step is to put all that energy back into you. Use these meditations at any point when you are feeling insecure, needy for affection or overwhelmed with emotions.

· AUDIO – EMOTIONAL CLEARING MEDITATION

Listen to this meditation on youtube

Guided Meditation Deep Emotional Clearing by Brian Scott

https://www.youtube.com/watch?v=5-MmGugM7GE

· **ART THERAPY ACTIVITY**

Draw the emotion that you are feeling in this moment. How would you represent this emotion if you could identify it within your body?

· **WRITTEN EXERCISE**

Write about the image you just made. What thoughts came up for you while you were drawing this image?

· **LIMERENCE**

If you are anxiously attached or in a codependent relationship you may identify with the tendency to put your romantic partner or crush on a pedestal and develop strong fantasies relating to them. You tend to see this romantic partner or crush as your rescuer, the person that will solve all your problems and fill your emotional, physical, or financial gaps. You may be idealizing this person so much that you feel that you need to be accepted by them, instead of judging if they are the right person for you.

Fantasies can be far reaching and take up a lot of time and mental space, distracting you from your work, family, and friends. Your anxious and fearful mind will create stories of how you will get together, have children, get married and start a family, even though the person is clearly showing you that they are not even close to starting a relationship with you or they keep promising that something will happen when it never does. However, your mind keeps this idealized relationship alive by creating fantasies that will prevent you from facing your worst fears; the relationship will never develop, the promises will not be kept, and your fantasy will never turn into reality.

Keeping the fantasy alive can be incredibly draining and painful because you invest a great deal of emotional intensity into it and then get disappointed when the fantasy does not come true. In this way continuing the cycle of ambivalence present in the anxious ambivalent attachment (intrusiveness/ unavailability). This is where the mental health aspect of the anxious attachment style comes in. A child will fantasize and idealize their parent while they are away, but once they are present will reject or feel uncomfortable in their presence. So, the fantasy keeps the good and comfortable feeling alive but at the same time continuing the cycle of unavailability and abandonment when the fantasy does not come true. People with anxious ambivalent attachment styles will also tend to feel bored when the other person starts exhibiting behaviors of reciprocity, interest, care, and affection. The fantasy and idealization of the other becomes more potent than dealing with the real person.

Limerence is the neurological term for the type of obsessive thinking and idealization of the other. It can be felt as a continuing loop of fantasies and obsessive thinking that your mind creates while trying to fill an emotional gap. It is difficult to get out of this cycle when you can't control your thoughts and they are paired with an emotion and intense need for affection.

Limerence is caused by different factors, neurochemistry, trauma bonding, attachment wounds, habits, and cultural and societal reinforcing of the love fantasy. From my point of view limerence is related to a deep need for affection and the constant searching for the love object, the source of care and affection, is equated to the longing and searching for the absent parent in the anxious ambivalent attachment style. The brain creates a fantasy to fill the gap because it does not know another way of sourcing affection. However, throughout these workshops you will learn how to source affection from yourself. See the **Healing from Childhood Trauma** and **Detach through Subconscious Reprogramming** sections to continue this process.

Fantasies are very powerful mindsets that will intuitively give you information about what you truly want and desire. For example, you desire a wedding, traveling having children and enjoying the company of a partner. However, the negative aspect is that you are projecting these desires onto the wrong person; a person who will never meet them. Through this written exercise you will learn how to use fantasies to your benefit and disconnect from them in order to stop the obsessive thinking.

· **WRITTEN EXERCISE**

Do this exercise before going to bed and when your brain is most open to receive and review information. Fantasies are powerful mindsets that will tell our subconscious what we truly want and desire. Through writing them out before bed you are telling your subconscious what you want and desire. Let's use them to your benefit!

Your unavailable romantic partner is only a projection through which your fantasy can come through. It does not mean that this fantasy will become true with them, but it may with another more suitable, healthy, and available partner.

Separate fantasy from reality. At the top of the page write FANTASY in bold capital letters. Under this heading write out all the fantasies you have with your romantic partner or crush. Write out every single detail and for everything out onto the pages until you can't think of any more fantasies. Put EVERYTHING down on paper without leaving anything out.

In another page write REALITY in big bold capital letters. Under this heading write out what is happening or has happened. You will notice a massive difference between the two.

Every time you have these fantasies or obsessive thinking write them out fully and if there is intense emotional distress attached to it use the Emotional Clearing written exercises above.

· DEALING WITH SEXUAL CRAVING

A very common symptom of codependency or an anxious ambivalent attachment style is an intense need for affection and sexual connection. We all have libido (sexual energy) that drives and motivates us to go for what we desire. However, it can be very difficult to control when you are also dealing with emotional symptoms, healing childhood trauma and have a deep need for affection and intimacy. The more you are in control of your sexuality through exploring yourself and setting boundaries with others, the more you will learn to control these impulses so that you only share sexual energy with the right person.

As I mentioned in the **Boundaries** chapter,not engaging sexually with the person you want to detach from is key to lasting emotional detachment and not falling into patterns where you are left feeling abandoned and rejected and the same time building self-worth. See the **Boundaries** chapter for more information on this.

The first step to dealing with sexual cravings is to make a promise or commitment to yourself to not engage sexually with the person you want to detach from or with anyone who is not exhibiting the traits of a healthy relationship. Second, exploring yourself sexually will relieve these symptoms as it will put you in a place of control and self-worth. You will be able to take care of your sexual needs without searching for satisfaction with the wrong person. Third, this deep need for affection comes from a childhood trauma or relationship trauma where physical affection, touch, caressing, warmth, and closeness was not provided. It can also stem from a sexual trauma, abuse neglect or an unhealthy sexuality from a previous partner. Go through the written exercises below to get to the root of the issue. A lot of emotions and confusion may come up through these exercises so be gentle and patient with yourself and if you feel the need contact a trusted friend or therapist for support.

DISCLAIMER: If you have been through a traumatic experience relating to sexuality, please seek professional help in the form of psychotherapy or with a licensed sex therapist as the information provided here does not replace this kind of treatment.

· **WRITTEN EXERCISE**

Write about your experience with sexuality. How did your parents teach you about sex and sexuality? Did you find out about sex through friends, family members, teachers, or parents? What beliefs do you have around sexuality? Write about the most memorable experiences, the most awkward, difficult, or pleasurable. What gives you pleasure? What do you enjoy in a sexual relationship? How do you envision a healthy sexual relationship?

· **CASUAL RELATIONSHIPS**

There is a tendency and a generational social normative that casual relationships will empower you to take control of your sexuality and enable you to get rid of the symptoms of codependency because you don't attach feelings to a relationship. The social norm says "it's only sex, enjoy yourself and forget about everything else. No strings attached, no emotional responsibility and no feelings." I really wish this were true! However, sexuality in humans is so complex and profound on a biological, social, cultural, religious, political, gender, cognitive, behavioral level that it makes it impossible for most of us for this to be true. I can only picture this norm being 100% true in reptiles where a sexual encounter is meant for procreation purposes only.

Sexuality is such a wide topic that I am sure there are individuals who live this norm and are comfortable and thriving exploring their sexuality in this manner. However, it only applies to a few with their own nuances in between. For the purposes of this chapter, we will explore what it means to the general public. Sexuality, sex and the physical encounter with the other *has meaning and it produces intense physical changes in our body's biochemistry **especially for women**_. See the **Boundaries** chapter for more information on this subject. Sexuality has so much meaning that poems, music, art theatre and literature and many more things are produced around this very subject every single day. So, there is no escaping the fact that a sexual encounter with another person will have an impact much further than just the satisfaction of a biological function.

During this process I strongly advice you not to get involved in casual relationships to alleviate the symptoms of codependency.

Engaging sexually with someone out of the need to feel affection, closeness and attention will only land you back on square one; where you are feeling abandoned, lonely, and rejected. Searching constantly for affection in a wide range of partners that do not show you any emotional responsibility or the care and affection that you fundamentally need, will further reinforce the belief imprinted through childhood trauma that you are not deserving of constant care, affection, and attention. And that this attention is fleeting and inconsistent.

If you do choose to engage in casual relationships out of curiosity and exploration, please keep in mind that it is just that and the relationship will most likely not be consistent and emotionally satisfying. For a relationship to develop there must be an emotional foundation that supports the physical connection, and these 4 items must be in place.

1. You have established that each person wants a committed relationship.
2. They are consistent in their actions and their words to-wards you.
3. You express your full self, and they meet this with support and love. They do the same with you.
4. You are exclusive to each other.

IV

RECOGNIZING YOUR TRAUMA TRIGGERS

6

What are trauma triggers?

Trauma triggers or emotional triggers are actions, situations, words, or experiences that create a deep sense of anxiety, sadness, confusion, negative body sensations and distress when you are confronted with them. This can happen with multiple people, not just with a romantic relationship. You can experience this with your boss, coworkers, teacher, mother, siblings etc. Emotional triggers can also be set off by smells, sounds, spaces, places, and situations.

A central part of this process is recognizing what exactly is triggering you about the way your partner, ex-partner or romantic crush is treating you. These triggers are emotional and therefore relate to a core wound that we experienced in childhood, this is why it so emotionally painful and difficult to detach from. Essentially your subconscious, and therefore your Central Nervous System, is telling you that it feels threatened and it reverts to that childhood situation. It is a natural defense mechanism that is deeply ingrained within our limbic system. However, there is no need to go into fight, flight, freeze or appease mode because our lives are not in danger. Therefore, this anxious feeling is purely psychological and emotional.

· WRITTEN EXERCISE

What behaviors, actions, words or situations about your crush, romantic partner or ex are triggering for you? Make a list in your journal and detail how they affect your mind and body. What specific childhood memory could they be related to? Add any new triggers that come up with any other person or situation. An example is given below.

"When I don't receive a text from my crush my chest tightens and I feel sadness, rejection and abandonment. This situation reminds me of the lack of communication with my mother."

· WRITTEN EXERCISE

Think of all the difficult situations or experiences that you went through during your childhood with your mother/father or caregivers. Below each experience write how it made you feel at that time. What were the beliefs that were imprinted during childhood? How did that experience have an impact on you today? What was the relationship between your parents like? Recognize your adverse childhood experiences (ACES) by writing fully about them and comparing them to the triggers you identified above. Do they match? How are they different?

Your experience is unique.

7

Breaking down childhood trauma

The symptoms of emotional codependency can vary in intensity from person to person depending on their **early childhood experiences and the beliefs** that were imprinted during this time, primarily from the ages of 0-7. As you learned in the **Psychology behind Emotional Attachment** chapter, emotional codependency stems from an anxious ambivalent attachment style.

Below you will find examples of adverse childhood experiences that will lead to an anxious ambivalent attachment style. Place a check mark or take note of the ones you identify with. The objective of this exercise is to identify and get to the root of those traumatic experiences so that you can later tackle them one by one through reprogramming.

- Inconsistent attention from parents or caregivers
- Intrusive behavior from parents or caregivers
- Abandoning or aloof parents or caregivers

· **DISCLAIMER**

Your childhood experiences may resemble some of these traits and not others. This is a general overview of the anxious/ambivalent attachment style and as mentioned before you may have traits from other attachment styles.

· **WRITTEN EXERCISE**

In a separate page in your journal, make a list of those situations that made you feel shame or emotional pain within your romantic relationship, crush or ex-partner, and see if you can trace them back to how your parents treated you in childhood based on the beliefs that you have about yourself today.

For example:

1. People pleasing- My parents criticized my ideas or achievements and therefore I created the belief that... what others think, feel and believe in is more important than what I think, feel or believe in.
2. Feeling rejected or abandoned - My parents were not present most of the time because they came home late from working all day and did not have time to play with me or listen to my concerns. Because of this I created the belief that I am not important and I am not deserving of love, affection or attention.

· **WRITTEN EXERCISE**

Copy the list and table below in your journal and write the beliefs that you have identified were imprinted in childhood due to the ACES (Adverse Childhood Experiences). Give yourself a new belief to reinforce what you are desiring. This is often the opposite of the limiting belief imprinted in childhood.

1. I don't deserve love
2. I will never find a partner
3. I'm not good enough
4. I don't deserve affection
5. I don't deserve attention
6. I don't deserve warm and loving communication
7. I can't trust others
8. I am always abandoned
9. I must do x to get affection
10. I am unlovable
11. I am not wanted
12. I don't deserve a healthy relationship
13. I must do x to get approval
14. I am not creative
15. I am not valued
16. I am not deserving
17. I am not worthy

1. Consciously reinforce this new belief daily when the trigger comes up or your brain defaults to it.

2. Write three new beliefs that you can reinforce today
3. Create an action plan with three actionable changes you are going to incorporate into your daily life to deepen the integration of the beliefs you have created from this exercise.

8

Linking present day triggers to childhood experiences

As you become aware of your emotions and how your partner or romantic crush triggers you, you will find similarities in how your parents treated you as a child and the beliefs that they imprinted in your subconscious.

For example, if your partner or romantic crush is triggering and abandoned or rejected emotion within you, then this means that somewhere in your childhood you also felt rejected and abandoned and the belief that was imprinted during childhood was "they don't care" or "I am not important." What makes this a problem is that despite having this overwhelming negative feeling that is being triggered by this person you still feel attracted to them and desire to be with them. This is because...

"The first relationship you have with parents, shapes your perception of what love is. So many of us don't see the red flags because they feel like home."

58

"When you get unhealthy behavior from a person but still feel attached to them, confusion will surely follow and this will inevitably trigger a childhood trauma wound that will send your body into dysregulation (fight, flight and freeze mode) vs. a rest and digest mode."

So, identifying the behaviors and situations that led to those beliefs is crucial to tackle them one by one during the reprogramming phase.

Learning to detach the emotional response

Learning to detach the emotional response from the person (toxic romantic partner or crush) is the key to eliminating the symptoms that are being projected through that person today.

So, the next time a person makes you feel abandoned, rejected or ashamed you will not attach to them or feel any attraction, on the contrary you will feel aversion, distaste and apathy. It will be an immediate turn off. Enabling you to detach from them and attach to the suitors that make you feel safe and loved.

Through this process you will learn that you are the owner of your emotions and through healing these childhood wounds you are able to detach the emotional response from that person. This is the key to detaching from codependency because your emotions no longer depend on what the other person does or says, you recognize them as your own. This is incredibly empowering! Learn how to get rid of your limiting beliefs and detach forever in the **Reprogramming your Subconscious chapter.**

· **ART THERAPY ACTIVITY**

Draw an image that represents your childhood self. You can represent them in any way, shape or form you want.

· **WRITTEN EXERCISE**

Write freely about the thoughts, ideas or emotions that came up for you during this activity. How did you represent your childhood self? What does this child need to feel more authentic, whole or loved?

VIDEO – ON MANAGING TRIGGERS

Listen to this video on youtube. Begin on minute 23:44 for the exercise.

Re Wire Your Triggers (Non Monogamy) by Jessica Fern

https://www.youtube.com/watch?v=Df6YcP4kHY4

V

DETACH THROUGH SUBCONSCIOUS REPROGRAMMING

10

Subconscious reprogramming

To fully disconnect the emotional response or trigger from your romantic partner or crush, overwrite old beliefs imprinted in childhood and create new beliefs, it is important to also reprogram the experience in your subconscious mind through repetition and emotional intensity. Through guided visualizations you will create new neural pathways that resemble a secure attachment style filled with love, affection, attention, and consistency. You will then take these positive new beliefs and make decisions based on them rather than the old low self-worth beliefs. Once you are making decisions based on the new beliefs you will be able to choose healthier and secure relationships while not recognizing the unhealthy and abusive relationships. In essence you will no longer trauma bond.

Have you ever asked yourself "Why are some people better at choosing high value partners instead of low value partners who constantly treat them badly day after day?" "Why do I continue to engage or pursue suitors or partners that don't

give me the time and attention that I deserve?"

For example, a child who had a secure attachment with their parents will have imprinted high self-worth beliefs during childhood and will only attach or bond to those partners that resemble secure attachments while not recognizing and not attaching to insecure, abusive or unavailable partners. Recognize your attachment style in the **Psychology behind Attachment** chapter and recognize your limiting beliefs that stem from Childhood Trauma in the **Healing from Childhood Trauma** chapter.

· **WRITTEN EXERCISE**

In your notebook write LIMITING BELIEFS as a title at the top of a new page. Below this title write all the limiting beliefs that emerged during the **Healing Childhood Trauma** chapter and add new ones each time they arise.

· **GUIDED MEDITATIONS**

The following guided meditation uses hypnosis and neuro-plasticity to overwrite old limiting beliefs and imprint new empowering beliefs. These guided meditations will gently put you into a rest and digest state that will immediately calm your central nervous system enabling for new information to be absorbed by your subconscious and your body. Through daily reinforcing you will able you to detach emotionally, physically and cognitively from a romantic crush, partner or suitor who is not in alignment with what you truly need and want, which is **a healthy relationship**.

Find a comfortable place where you will not be disturbed for about 20 - 40 minutes. Use a blanket and an eye pillow to cover your eyes for the meditations as this will allow you to put your whole body and mind into a restful semi sleep.

· **AUDIO – INNER CHILD GUIDED MEDITATION**

Inner Child Guided Meditation by the Holistic Psychologist

https://www.youtube.com/watch?v=tyGMZU5DfNs

· **ART THERAPY ACTIVITY**

Draw an image that represents safety, love and connection. What does secure attachment look like for you in a relationship?

· **WRITTEN EXERCISE**

What thoughts, ideas or emotions came up for you during the art making process? How does your image represent safety, connection and affection?

VI

FINDING YOUR IDEAL PARTNER

11

Do the work first

To enter the dating process, which is basically a process of selecting the right person for you. It is important that you learn about **attachment styles** and how they influence the way you select your partner. Attachment styles are the ways in which, as children we learned how to love, care for, bond or attach to others through how our parents or main caregivers loved, cared for us or bonded with us. So, we basically learned how to relate to others through how our parents or caregivers related to us. These attachment patterns were imprinted into our subconscious, and we integrated them as true beliefs. There are four types of attachments styles; three of them are insecure attachment (anxious/ambivalent, avoidant/dismissive and disorganized) One of them is a secure attachment

Please view **The Psychology behind Attachment** chapter to identify your attachment style and then go through the other chapters in order to reprogram any limiting beliefs and any childhood trauma that could potentially influence how you behave in a relationship. This is such an important part of the process because it will determine the kind of partner you choose and the dynamic of the relationship. Please view the **Dealing with the Symptoms** chapter to learn more about how to deal with codependency symptoms and engaging in casual relationships.

12

What makes up a healthy relationship

I am guessing that if you are reading this book you want to find a long-term relationship and are interested in working towards this. According to Drs. John and Julie Gottman (gottman.com) there are some key differences that separate a relationship success from a relationship failure, and it is important to keep this is in mind when you are beginning the dating process. These are key elements to keep in mind when you are getting to know someone.

The key elements that separate healthy relationships from unhealthy relationships are:

- Partners who emphasized the positive traits of each other instead of the negative traits
- Fondness, affection, and admiration
- We-ness vs. separateness
- Expansiveness vs. withdrawal

- Glorifying the struggle
- Compassionate, loving and empathic communication

The other elements that Drs. John and Julie Gottman (gottman.com) identified make up a healthy relationship are coming to agreements about the following topics:

1. Trust and Commitment
2. Addressing Conflict
3. Sex and Intimacy
4. Work and money
5. Family
6. Fun and adventure
7. Growth and spirituality
8. Dreams

TRUST AND COMMITMENT

Commitment in relationships means choosing your partner every day. Trust is built with this daily commitment.

Use the following premises to reflect on how you and your partner relate to each other

- You invest emotionally in this relationship
- You choose to resist possibilities with others that break trust in the relationship and maintain healthy boundaries with

others for the same purpose.

- If you feel discomfort in your relationship you communicate with your partner instead of complaining to someone else.
- You accept your partner completely, including his or her flaws.
- You value the relationship you have and encourage gratitude.
- You don't threaten to leave the relationship
- you care about your partner's pain just as much as your own.

Trust is lost when:

- You don't prioritize your partner
- You break promises
- You are not present when your partner needs you
- You lie, keep secrets or are unfaithful

Ask yourself:

- Do you trust your partner?
- Would you be available when they needed you?
- Are you loyal?
- How important are they to you?

ADDRESSING CONFLICT

It is impossible to have a relationship without conflicts. Conflicts in relationships will always happen. It is the way the couple manages to resolve conflicts that really puts you in the category of successful relationships.

Use the following premises to reflect on how you and your partner relate to each other.

- Problems that have solutions deal with a specific situation or topic.
- Perpetual problems deal with fundamental differences in personality or lifestyle. All couples have perpetual problems, and they make up 69% of the conflicts that happen between couples.
- Some perpetual problems do not have a definitive solution, but the couple usually creates a tolerance and get used to them or generate tools to live with them.
- Some perpetual problems have no solution, and the couple enters a dynamic of "gridlock" where no one gives in, and each one is fixed in their position.
- Make a list of conflicts that have arisen with your partner and write about how you have resolved them.

Ask yourself:

- How did you handle conflict in your family?
- How was rage or anger expressed in your family?
- How can your partner support you when you feel rage and anger?
- How do you like to resolve things after a conflict?
- What have you learned about your partner because of con-

flict?

SEX AND INTIMACY

Sexuality is an important element within the relationship. If there is a lack of physical affection, flirtation or intimate connection other than sex, the couple's sexual life suffers. If there is emotional distance or intense conflict, the couple's sexual life suffers. If there is a lack of emotional or physical security or someone does not feel appreciated, it can affect the quality and quantity of a couple's sexual life. Giving and receiving "sexual feedback" after every sexual encounter will help to alleviate some of these issues.

Use the following premises to reflect on how you and your partner relate to each other.

- Romantic and intimate rituals maintain the connection and passion between the couple.
- Couples who can talk openly about sex have more sex and women have more orgasms.
- Talking about sex is difficult for most couples, but it gets easier with time and practice.
- Tell your partner what they do well and what you like and not what they are doing wrong.
- Normal sexuality is what the couple decides feels good.

Ask yourself:

- Think about all the times you have had sex with your partner. What have been the best moments? What things about that moment did you like?
- What things excite you?
- How do you think you can increase your partner's passion?
- How would you like them to tell you that they want to have sex with you?
- Where and how would you like to be touched?
- What is your favorite place to have sex and why?
- Is there something sexual you've always wanted to try, but never asked?
- How often would you like to have sex?
- What can your partner do to improve your sex life?

WORK AND MONEY

Money is one of the 5 elements that cause conflict in a couple. Each person has a history and family values that were instilled in each one around this topic. The goal of each person is to understand their partner and not define or change the other so that they have the same values. Work life is the other commitment, apart from marriage and family, that significantly influences a couple's relationship.

Use the following premises to reflect on how you and your partner relate to each other.

- The difficulty with money relates to the meaning it has for each person.

- Sharing housework is a fundamental part of a successful relationship.
- Work life and earning money is like a third person in the relationship, demanding time and energy.
- Having a balance in your relationship and your work life is essential for the success of your relationship.
- If a person has a lot of work stress and works long hours, it will create isolation and a lack of emotional connection that ends up damaging the relationship.
- Discovering what money means to both of you will help resolve conflicts you may have around money.
- It is important to foster gratitude for what you have and the contribution each makes to the relationship.

Ask yourself:

- How do you feel in your work life?
- How do you imagine your work environment changing in the future?
- What is your biggest fear around money?
- What do you need to feel confident when you talk about how you spend your money or how you get money?
- What is your biggest concern around money?
- What are your dreams and aspirations with money?
- How would you like to share money with your partner?
- How do you think your work life affects your relationship?

FAMILY

Talking about whether to have children is essential to establish the viability of a relationship. If one person wants to have children and the other does not, it may mean that the relationship is not viable. The number of children, at what age and whether they come from recomposed families, are important variables to consider in relation to the success of a couple.

Use the following premises to reflect on how you and your partner relate to each other.

- The definition of a family is diverse and can include children, adopted children, stepchildren, no children, pets, friends, relatives or extended family. –
- Honesty when telling your partner whether you want to have children or not is very important since it is not advisable to enter a relationship with the idea that you will be able to convince your partner to have children or not to have children.
- Consider the costs of having a child. Calculate the costs of food, education, care, medicine, etc.
- The couple's relationship is more important than the relationship that the couple has with their children.
- Approximately 2/3 of couples have a significant drop in relationship satisfaction after the birth of a child and this drop becomes increasingly significant with each child they have.
- To alleviate marital dissatisfaction after having a child, it is important for parents to be involved in the pregnancy, birth,

and care of the baby. During this time conflict should be kept to a minimum and sexual relations must be maintained.

Ask yourself:

- How do you imagine your ideal family? Just the couple? Friends and family?
- How many children do you want to have?
- How do you think your relationship would change after having children?
- What problems might arise around sex life and intimacy after having children?
- What excites you about being a parent?
- What characteristics do you think your children would have about you/the other?
- How would you create a sense of family without children?
- Who in your family or friends could you consider part of the family?

FUN AND ADVENTURE

The ability to play, have fun, and go on adventures is essential to creating meaning within the relationship. Experiences with friends, family or children visiting places, traveling and experimenting allow the couple to get to know each other in different spaces, creating bonds of connection and meaning within the relationship. Relationships begin to deteriorate when the elements of play, novel experiences or shared adventures do not exist. Therefore, the relationship becomes a series of mundane tasks that make the couple question the purpose of the relationship.

Use the following premises to reflect on how you and your partner relate to each other

- Play and novel experiences are essential components of a successful and joyful relationship.
- The need for adventure is deeply rooted in our brain and is part of the brain's "Reward System."
- When we experience new things we receive a rush of dopamine, the happiness hormone.
- It's okay if your partner has a different idea of what adventure or novel experiences are. The key is to respect each other's sense of adventure and what it means to your partner.
- Play and novel experiences build trust, intimacy, and a sense of connection.

Ask yourself:

- What does novel experiences, play or adventure mean to you?
- How did you like to play or experience new things when you were a child?
- Do you remember any adventures or novel experiences you've had in the last year?
- How do you think you can involve more play in your rela-

tionship?
- Make a list of experiences or plans that you would like to carry out with your partner.

GROWTH AND SPIRITUALITY

Each person has a series of beliefs about themselves and the world around them that help them create meaning in their lives. These types of beliefs translate into the personal development and spirituality of each person. Beliefs, rituals and personal development, influence the routines and lifestyle of the couple. The goal is not for the couple to have the same beliefs, but for them to benefit, value and learn how they
are different.

Use the following premises to reflect on how you and your partner relate to each other

Ask yourself:

- What types of routines and rituals influence your relation-ship?
- Are there philosophical, religious or cultural beliefs that influence your relationship?
- How would you like to celebrate anniversaries, birthdays and Christmas with your partner?
- What type of personal development activities are you implementing in your daily life that you think influence your partner?

- Make a list of beliefs that you live by in your life and share them with your partner.
- What things do you consider sacred in your personal life?
- What kind of spiritual beliefs do you want to instill in your children?

DREAMS

Every person has dreams and aspirations about things they want to achieve in their life. It is important that in relationships each person feels supported in the goals and objectives they want to achieve. In some situations, these dreams get in the way of the relationship and cause the couple to distance themselves. In other situations, the couple manages to support each other by dedicating their time and space in areas that allow their partner to pursue their dreams.

Use the following premises to reflect on how you and your partner relate to each other

- Honoring your partner's dreams is one of the secret ingredients of successful couples.
- Each person has dreams and aspirations apart from the relationship.
- No one should sacrifice their dreams, goals or objectives for their relationship.
- It is important to share your dreams, goals and objectives with your partner and communicate the ways in which they can support you in achieving them.

Ask yourself:

- What are your dreams and aspirations?
- How can you support your partner with their dreams, goals and aspirations?
- What kind of dreams, goals and aspirations are common between you and your partner?
- What types of words or actions tell you that your partner is supporting you in achieving your dreams?
- How would you like your partner to support you in achieving your dreams?

SELECTING THE IDEAL PARTNER

Below, you will find a checklist that will help you determine if it is a relationship that has the potential to last or not.

A healthy relationship is reciprocal and mutual: it means that both people exhibit these characteristics for at least 6 months

- Consistency and confidence; words match actions
- The relationship and you are a priority in their life
- Your partner makes you feel safe and loved
- They clearly express their needs and boundaries
- They don't make you feel guilty or ashamed
- They make you notice your weaknesses or difficulties with love

- They care about you and how their behavior impacts you.
- They talk about a future together and you are part of that plan
- If there is a conflict, they try to repair it and do everything possible to reach an agreement with you.
- Their love, affection and attention feel unconditional, but there is respect for boundaries in time and space
- Your partner is flexible and can reach agreements with you

13

Conclusion

I n the journey through the pages of this book, we've explored the depths of heartbreak, navigating its twists and turns with courage and resilience. We've uncovered the raw emotions, faced the painful truths, and embraced the healing power within. As we reach the conclusion, let us remember that healing is not a destination but a transformative process, a journey of self-discovery and growth.

Throughout this book we have arrived at a synthesis of empirical findings and therapeutic strategies that illuminate the path towards healing from heartbreak. Drawing from psychological theories, therapeutic modalities, and evidence-based practices, we have delineated a comprehensive roadmap for individuals traversing the tumultuous terrain of emotional recovery.

Through the lens of cognitive-behavioral interventions, we have explored the intricate interplay between thoughts, emotions, and behaviors in the context of heartbreak. By challenging maladaptive beliefs and restructuring cognitive schemas, you can cultivate resilience and foster adaptive coping mechanisms to navigate the aftermath of romantic loss.

Furthermore, the integration of mindfulness-based approaches has offered profound insights into the cultivation of self-awareness, acceptance, and compassion amidst the throes of heartache. Through mindfulness practices such as meditation, self-compassion exercises, and emotional regulation techniques, you can cultivate a present-focused orientation that fosters emotional equilibrium and facilitates the processing of grief.

Moreover, the therapeutic exploration of attachment dynamics and interpersonal relationships has shed light on the profound impact of attachment experiences of heartbreak. By fostering a deeper understanding of attachment styles, you can gain insight into their relational patterns and cultivate healthier, more fulfilling relationships in the aftermath of romantic loss.

The journey of healing from heartbreak is multifaceted and nuanced, encompassing cognitive, emotional, and relational dimensions. By synthesizing empirical research with clinical insights, this book offers a comprehensive framework for individuals seeking to transcend the pain of romantic loss and embark on a journey of self-discovery, growth, and resilience.

As we close this chapter, let us carry forward the knowledge that healing is a testament to the resilience of the human spirit. Let us embrace each day with hope and gratitude, knowing that with each sunrise, we are one step closer to wholeness. May this book serve as a beacon of light for those navigating the shadows of heartbreak, guiding them towards a future filled with love, joy, and boundless possibilities.

owlby, John. (2006). *Vínculos afectivos. Formación, desarrollo y pérdida.*

Bowlby, John. (1983). *Attachment and Loss.*

Bernstein, Gabrielle. (2022) *Happy Days: The guided path from trauma to profound freedom and inner peace.*

Burns, David. (2020) *Feeling great: the revolutionary new treatment for depression and anxiety.*

Dehlia, Lala. (2019) *Vibrate higher daily.*

Fern, Jessica. (2020). *Polysecure: Attachment, Trauma and Consensual Nonmonogamy.*

Gottman, John & Schwartz Gotman, Julie. (2019) *Eight dates. Essential Conversations for a lifetime of love.*

Kerner, Ian. (2021). *So tell me about the last time you had sex. Laying bare and learning to repair our love lives.*

Kerner, Ian. (2004). *She comes first.The thinking man's guide to pleasuring a woman.*

Lepera, Nicole. (2021) *How to do the work: Recognize your patterns, heal from your past and create yourself.*

Levine, Amir & Heller S.F, Rachel. (2011). *Attached: The new science of adult attachment and how it can help you find and keep love.*

Perel, Esther. (2019). *The couple's dilemma.*

Perel, Esther. (2009). *Erotic Intelligence.*

15

About the Author

Viviana Molina

Viviana has professional training as an Art Psychotherapist from Goldsmiths, University of London, and as a Psychologist from the Universidad de Los Andes in Bogotá, Colombia.

Viviana has worked as an Art Therapist, Psychologist, and educator of artistic processes with children, adolescents, and adults in the areas of mental, educational, and social health. She dedicates her spare time to publishing books about mental health.

16

Books by Viviana

Heal Heartbreak in 5 steps Workbook (to be used with "Heal Heartbreak in 5 steps book)

Desapego y Amor propio Cuaderno de Trabajo (para ser utilizado con el libro Desapego y Amor Propio en 5 pasos) Spanish edition

Desapego y Amor Propio en 5 pasos Cuaderno de trabajo (para ser utilizado con el libro "Desapego y Amor Propio en 5 Pasos")
Spanish edition

17

Review

Thanks for reading my book! I hope you enjoyed it and have benefited from the information and exercises contained within. If you liked the book and would like to support me in furthering my publishing business, please head over to the Amazon page and leave a review! If you have any questions, doubts or would like to book a virtual session please email me at vivianamolin@gmail.com

www.ingramcontent.com/pod-product-compliance
Lightning Source LLC
Chambersburg PA
CBHW052113150726
48002CB00006B/2328